KU-708-159

To a very special
GRANDPA

Written by Pam Brown
Illustrations by Juliette Clarke

Every grandfather is different, but a
really good grandfather has a lot in
common with all the other good
grandfathers. Kindliness and
cuddliness, stories and an inclination
to take one's side.

. . .

⧉EXLEY
NEW YORK • WATFORD, UK

"GRANDPA" MEANS LOVE

Grandad, Grandpapa, Grandy, Gangan, Pop.
All names of love.

. . .

The love between grandchildren and their
grandfather is a precious thing – an exchange of
gifts before the young head out to sea and the old
seek their safe haven. The meeting may be brief, or
long and full of joy – but each transforms the other.
Each is richer for the touch of hands and the shared
laughter. Each lives forever in the other's heart.

. . .

You do not need to speak when we meet each other.
You hug me tight and I am home.

. . .

If every child had a grandfather as wise
and sensible, kind and patient, forgiving
and firm-minded, interesting and clever
and encouraging as you – there would
be no more trouble in the world.
Anywhere.

. . .

Grandfathers have loving hearts.
That is why a grandfather never ever blanches when
his grandchild toddles toward him with a beaming
smile and a beautiful bunch of flowers he was
nurturing for Saturday's Flower Show.

. . .

TIME TOGETHER

Going on a bus with most people is
going on a bus.
Going on a bus with Grandad
is an adventure.

. . .

A grandchild likes to take Grandad's hands and
escape from the house after lunch, when the dirty
dishes need washing. Grandads need no persuasion!

. . .

A day out with Grandpa usually ends
with him saying,
"I wouldn't tell your mother – it's just between us two."
This covers far too much ice cream, strange seafood,
a sip of Grandpa's beer, the roller-coaster he's been
forbidden, a small bet on a poker game – and such.

. . .

Grandads steel themselves to games of crazy golf
and rowing round the lake, to rescuing
grandchildren from the top of slides, to building
castles on the beach, to turning every handle in the
museum's children's gallery, to feeding pigeons
in the park.
But they wilt a little on the third time round.

. . .

There is no happier sight than a grandad and a
grandchild engaged in a furious polka.

. . .

SPECIAL GRANDADS

Grandads come in every shape and size.

Tall grandads – a tree to climb, a peak to

conquer, a launching pad to outer space.

Rotund grandads. Teddy bears grown human size,

to kiss and cuddle.

Great, square-shouldered grandads to roar

you round the garden, to stride you over

moorland, to carry you home under

the pin bright stars.

Small grandads, who talk quietly to you for hours

and who fit inside your secret den and

see things from your point of view.

Floppy grandads, to drowse on by the fire.

Clever grandads who know everything there is to know – and who are on nodding terms with all the gallery attendants.

Quiet grandads, who call the sparrows to their fingers with gentle whistlings ....or walk you through the summer woods.

All dear. All wise. All loving.

But none so much as mine.

. . .

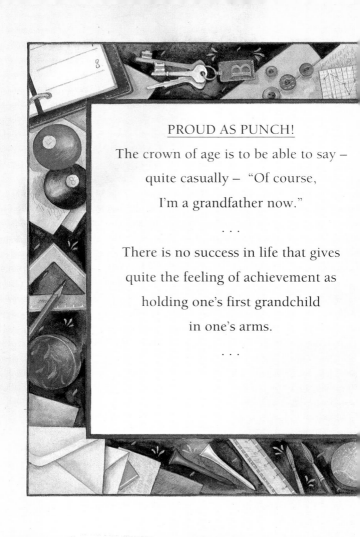

PROUD AS PUNCH!

The crown of age is to be able to say –
quite casually – "Of course,
I'm a grandfather now."

. . .

There is no success in life that gives
quite the feeling of achievement as
holding one's first grandchild
in one's arms.

. . .

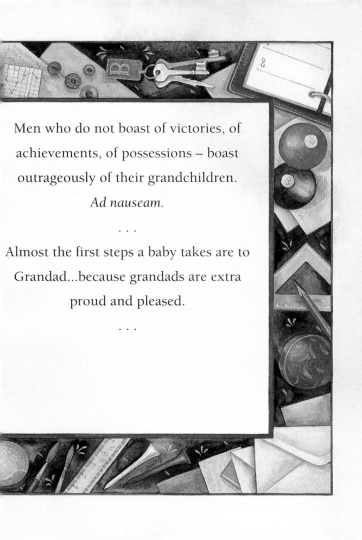

Men who do not boast of victories, of achievements, of possessions – boast outrageously of their grandchildren. *Ad nauseam.*

. . .

Almost the first steps a baby takes are to Grandad...because grandads are extra proud and pleased.

. . .

I don't know how I would grow
up without Grandpa.
He knows the route, you see.

. . .

The applause was fine.
But the accolade was a
grandfather's hug and "I told you,
you could do it!"

. . .

Every child in the world has
something special to give. Often it
is the grandpa who spots it first.

. . .

GUIDING AND ENCOURAGING ME

Thank you for showing me, very carefully, very patiently, how to do things.

And not even sighing when I get it wrong yet again. "Never mind. That was much better. You're getting there. Have another go."

. . .

Whenever I do something I am proud of – the crown is to know your delight in it.

. . .

Thank you for letting me ride my hobby horses on issues that are your particular specialities – and putting me right so gently that I think I've amended my argument all on my own.

. . .

Grandpa you don't need to do much – just be there.

. . .

NOISY! DARING! FUN!

There's really nothing quite like a grandad on the spree. They are noisier, happier, greedier and far more daft than any kid. It's best to give up being dignified – and go down the helter-skelter, too.

. . .

Grandads have had to be sensible most of their lives. Now's the time to unbutton.

. . .

A man's children look at one another and say – "Did you know he could do the sand-dance?... Balance things on his chin?... Wiggle his ears?... Yodel?" He's been saving it up for his grandchildren.

. . .

Grandads have won the right to be a little eccentric. It makes one look forward to getting old.

. . .

Grandads no longer listen to people who tell them
how to live.
They take no notice of fashion. They pick and
choose the rules they will obey.
They are very comfortable.
And make the grandchildren feel very
comfortable, too.

. . .

OUR PROTECTOR

Where should we be without you, Grandad?
You hold the whole family in your arms.
Whatever our differences, whatever our
squabbles, we are united in your love.
Hold us tight, Grandad.
Hold us safe.

. . .

Thank you for dropping everything in an
emergency and coming at a run. Thank you
for turning your hand to anything. Thank
you for staying calm and sensible when
everyone else was gibbering.
Thank you for seeing us through.

. . .

When I am afraid, I like to be with you.

Because you have often been afraid – you've told me so.

And it all came right in the end.

. . .

When everyone is yelling at you, grandads thump you very gently on the head and just say "idiot".

And smile.

And at once you see that's exactly what you've been.

. . .

When we go anywhere busy, noisy or scary – I like to hold your hand tight.

It's the safest, most comforting hand I know.

. . .

<u>SHARING</u>

There's nowhere more comfortable for a small

child to have a nap than on the knees of a

sleeping grandad.

. . .

We need each other, you and I.

You to tell me about the Long Ago

and me to tell you how computers work.

. . .

Grandfathers and grandchildren suit each other.

. . .

Grandfathers were once small children, teenagers,
lovers, newly-weds, young parents. They have
known many joys, many troubles, been tossed by
circumstances, suffered loss and disappointment
and fear, tasted success, changed with the
passing years.

They remember – and, in remembering, share the
lives of everyone, from the oldest son or daughter to
the smallest grandchild.

Times may change, but every grandfather
can sit down quietly with any one of his
family and say with honesty,
"I know. I know. I understand."

Or take their hands and shout with joy and
say, "I am so glad for you. Because I remember...."

. . .

MEMORIES

It's good when we're out walking to hold your hand

and to know that this same hand held Daddy's,

when he was the same age as me.

. . .

I treasure all the things we've done together, Grandpa. I'll write them in my diary – and paste the photographs beside them. So that I'll remember it all – and my children who will follow will know a little of the joy we've known in one another's company, and be happy to have such people in their past.

. . .

Dear Grandpa

Write it all down. Please. All the things that seem so ordinary – things you thought, when you were small, would never change. For they have changed and are still changing and soon will exist only in your memory.

Write them down for me.

And for my children.

And my children's children.

. . .

ALWAYS

We'll sit here in the sun and eat our sandwiches and
watch the gulls soar and circle overhead – and
talk, and smile.
It is a summer afternoon we've taken out of time –
one that we'll have forever.

. . .

You have been a part of my life since I can
remember – your eyes smiling, your hands stretched
to steady and guide me, your arms quick to keep me
from any danger and to rock me into sleep.
I have ridden your shoulders, clasped your hand,
shared small adventures.
Listened to your stories. Laughed at your jokes.
Wondered at your magic.
You are a part of my life.
You are a part of me.
Till the end of time.

. . .

Thank you for
seeing all our
childish gifts for
what they truly are
– expressions of
our love.
And keeping them
among your
treasures.

<u>FOR EVERYTHING...</u>

Thank you for keeping my secrets solemnly and well. Thank you for listening to my tales of woe with patience and a grave attention. Thank you for bringing my white mouse to see me in hospital.... Thank you for listening to my jokes and saying, "very good!" Thank you for slipping me a coin or two – "To tide you over." Thank you for assuring me that cats have quite as good a chance of Heaven as anyone else. Thank you for teaching me the Slow March and Present Arms, and how to hone boots to a liquid shine. Thank you for treating me as a fellow expert. Thank you for getting me out of bed, when all the rest were sleeping, to see a shower of falling stars. Thank you for mending things before my parents found out. Thank you for being my friend – for now and always.

. . .

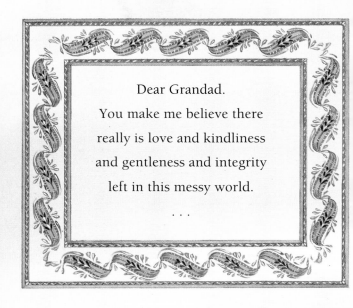

Dear Grandad.
You make me believe there
really is love and kindliness
and gentleness and integrity
left in this messy world.

. . .

THE THINGS THAT MATTER

Grandads have mostly discovered that love and
friendship far outweigh all the rest of living.
It's the greatest wisdom they can pass on.
If only we'd listen.

. . .

You have taught me the one essential thing.
That the world is made up of grandmas
and grandpas,
fathers and mothers, children and grandchildren.
Not of Serbs and Croats, Jews and Gentiles, Hindus
and Moslems, Catholics and Protestants, blacks and
whites and yellows.
Just families. Just people.

. . .

Human beings learn about love as they go along.
They only just get it sorted out in time
for the grandchildren.

. . .

Grandfathers have found out the hard way what
matters and what doesn't.
A pair of small arms wound about the neck, a
splodgy kiss – "I luff you, Grandpa" – are far more
valuable than the decisions of the Board.

. . .